PALEO COOKBOOK

LUNCH EDITION

Paleo Lunch Recipes
with Easy Instructions

Jamie Evans

© Copyright 2021 - All rights reserved.

TABLE OF CONTENTS

PORK CUTLETS WITH BABY TRUSS TOMATOES

Take one baking tray, add ingredients, slide it into a warm oven and let the flavors mingle as meat becomes golden and vegies turn crisp on the outside and tender on the inside.

INGREDIENTS

6 pork cutlets

2 tablespoons Cajun seasoning

1 tablespoon olive oil

1 large red onion, halved, cut into wedges

6 Lebanese eggplants, halved lengthways

3 **zucchini**, quartered lengthways

Olive oil spray

2 red apples, halved, cored, cut into thick wedges

2 x 275g pkts baby roma truss tomatoes

METHOD

STEP 1

Preheat oven to 200°C. Sprinkle both sides of pork with the seasoning. Heat the oil in a large heavy-based flameproof roasting pan over medium heat. Cook the pork for 2 minutes each side or until golden. Transfer to a plate.

STEP 2

Place the onion, eggplant and zucchini in the pan. Spray with oil and season with salt and pepper. Roast for 15 minutes or until the vegetables just start to soften.

STEP 3

Arrange the pork, apple and tomatoes in the pan with the vegetables. Roast, using a spoon to remove any excess liquid from the pan halfway through cooking, for a further 20 minutes.

NUTRITION VALUE

1028 KJ Energy, 9g fat, 1g saturated fat, 5g fiber, 33g protein, 12g carbs.

PALEO ALMOND, PECAN AND COCONUT CRUMBED CHICKEN

Baked chicken with a nutty, crunchy coating served with a warm vege salad ticks all the boxes for a healthy, Paleo-friendly meal.

INGREDIENTS

1/2 cup natural almonds

1/3 cup pecans

1/2 cup shredded coconut

3 teaspoons lemon rind,

1 garlic clove, quartered

1 egg, lightly beaten

1 tablespoon water, cold

4 small **Chicken Breasts**

1 tablespoon macadamia oil

250g Brussels sprouts,

1 large head broccoli,

1 tablespoon pine nuts

1 tablespoon pepitas

1 tablespoon sunflower kernels

1/2 avocado, roughly chopped

1/4 cup apple cider vinegar

2 tablespoons macadamia oil

1 teaspoon Dijon mustard

METHOD

STEP 1

Preheat oven to 180C/160C fan-forced. Line a baking tray with baking paper. Process almonds, pecans, coconut, lemon rind and garlic in a food processor until finely chopped. Transfer to a large shallow bowl. Season with salt and pepper. Whisk egg and water in a shallow bowl until combined. Dip chicken in egg mixture, then press in nut mixture to coat all over. Transfer to prepared tray. Drizzle with oil. Bake for 30 minutes

STEP 2

Meanwhile, make Broccoli and sprout salad: Cook Brussels sprouts in a large saucepan of boiling water for 2 minutes or until just starting to turn bright green. Transfer to a large bowl of iced water. Repeat with broccoli. Heat a small frying pan over medium high heat. Cook pine nuts, pepitas and sunflower seeds for 3 to 4 minutes or until toasted. Drain sprouts and broccoli. Transfer to a large bowl. Add avocado and pine nut mixture. Whisk vinegar, oil, mustard and dill in a jug. Season with salt and pepper. Drizzle over salad.

NUTRITION VALUE

1190 KJ Energy, 20g fat,
7g fiber, 46.8g protein, 5.8g carbs.

PORK AND SWEET POTATO SKEWERS

Recipe that everyone love.

MAKES 4 SERVING/ TOTAL TIME 65 MINUTE

INGREDIENTS

500g orange sweet potato, peeled, cubed

600g **pork fillet**, cubed

2 tbsp olive oil

1 tbsp ground cumin

1/3 cup wholegrain mustard

Chopped chives, to serve

Apple sauce, to serve

METHOD

STEP 1

Place potato and 2 tablespoons water in a heatproof, microwave-safe bowl. Microwave, covered, on high (100%) for 4 to 5 minutes or until just tender. Drain. Set aside to cool.

STEP 2

Thread pork and potato onto 8 skewers. Place in a dish. Drizzle with oil. Sprinkle with cumin. Turn to coat.

STEP 3

Preheat a barbecue plate or chargrill on medium heat. Cook skewers, turning occasionally, for 6 to 8 minutes or until pork is cooked through and potato is browned. Remove to a plate. Set aside, covered, for 5 minutes to rest.

STEP 4

Brush skewers with mustard. Sprinkle with chives. Serve with apple sauce.

NUTRITION VALUE

1450 KJ Energy, 12g fat, 2g saturated fat, 3 fiber, 37 Protein, 12g carbs.

PORK AND EGGPLANT PARMIGIANA

This tasty pork and eggplant parmigiana recipe can be made ahead of time and will have all the family asking for more!

INGREDIENTS

1 cup (75g) panko breadcrumbs

1/4 cup (20g) finely grated parmesan

1 garlic clove, crushed

1 tbs flat-leaf parsley, finely chopped

2 Coles Australian Free Range Eggs, lightly whisked

2 x 400g pkts Coles Australian Pork Sizzle Steak*

Olive oil, to shallow-fry

1 large eggplant, sliced crossways

500g Coles Mum's Sause Garden Veg

200g mozzarella, sliced

Green salad, to serve

METHOD

STEP 1

Place the breadcrumbs, parmesan, garlic and parsley in a shallow bowl and stir to combine. Season. Place the egg in a separate shallow bowl. Dip 1 pork steak in the egg, then in the breadcrumb mixture and turn to coat. Transfer to a plate. Repeat, in batches, with the remaining pork, egg and breadcrumb mixture. Add enough oil to a large frying pan to come 1cm up the side of the pan. Heat over medium heat. Cook the pork, in batches, for 3 mins each side or until the pork is golden and cooked through. Transfer to a plate.

STEP 2

Add enough oil to the frying pan to come 1cm up the side. Heat over medium-high heat. Cook the eggplant, in batches, for 1 min each side or until golden brown. Transfer to another plate lined with paper towel. Preheat grill on high. Line a large baking tray with foil. Place the pork on the lined tray. Spoon the pasta sauce evenly over the pork. Top with the eggplant and mozzarella. Cook under the grill for 5 mins or until mozzarella melts and is golden. Divide the pork mixture and salad evenly among serving plates. Season.

NUTRITION VALUE

1937 KJ Energy, 20g fat, 7g saturated fat, 3g fiber, 45g protein, 15g carbs.

SALMON WITH MANGO & CHILLI SALSA

Bursting with goodness, this low-fat recipe fuses sweet fruit with fresh vegies - perfect for a warm summer day or evening.

INGREDIENTS

1 tbsp olive oil

4 (about 220g each) skinless **salmon** fillets

2 ripe mangoes, cheeks removed, peeled, finely chopped

1 long fresh red chili, halved, deseeded, thinly sliced

2 tbsp chopped fresh coriander

1 tbsp fresh lime juice

1 bunch asparagus, woody ends trimmed

Lime wedges, to serve

METHOD

STEP 1

Heat oil in a non-stick frying pan over medium-high heat. Season salmon with salt and pepper. Cook for 3-4 minutes each side or until just cooked through.

STEP 2

Meanwhile, combine the mango, chili, coriander and lime juice in a bowl. Taste and season with salt and pepper.

STEP 3

Cook the asparagus in a saucepan of boiling water for 2-3 minutes or until bright green and tender crisp.

STEP 4

Divide the salmon among serving plates. Top with asparagus and salsa and serve with lime wedges.

NUTRITION VALUE

2100 KJ Energy, 20g fat, 5g saturated fat, 2g fiber, 55g protein, 11g carbs.

ROAST CHICKEN THIGH FILLETS

Use these tasty roast chicken thighs as a base for some great family meals such as stir-fries, pastas and pies.

MAKES 8 SERVING/ TOTAL TIME 25 MINUTE

INGREDIENTS

8 x 150g **chicken thigh** fillets

2 tablespoons olive oil

METHOD

STEP 1

Preheat oven to 180°C/160°C fan-forced. Place chicken in a large roasting pan. Drizzle with oil. Toss to coat chicken in oil. Season with salt and pepper.

STEP 2

Roast for 20 minutes or until chicken is cooked though. Allow to cool before refrigerating.

NUTRITION VALUE

1081 KJ Energy, 17g fat, 4g saturated fat, 26g protein, 13.5g carbs.

OLIVE & HERB FISH PARCELS

Recipe that Everyone love.

MAKES 4 SERVING/ TOTAL TIME 20 MINUTE

INGREDIENTS

120g baby spinach leaves

4 blue-eye fillets, deboned

2 **zucchini**, sliced

40 small black olives

120ml extra virgin olive oil

2 tablespoons lemon juice

2 teaspoons grated lemon rind

1 garlic clove, finely chopped

1 tablespoon finely chopped mint

2 tablespoons finely chopped basil

1 tablespoon finely chopped chives

METHOD

STEP 1

Preheat the oven to 190°C.

STEP 2

Cut four 30cm sheets of foil and lay on work surface. Cut 4 sheets of baking paper the same size and place on top of foil.

STEP 3

Divide spinach between parcels, then place a fish fillet on top. Divide zucchini and olives between parcels. Use a total of 2 tablespoons of the olive oil to drizzle onto fish. Season with salt and pepper.

STEP 4

Place remaining oil in a small bowl, whisk in lemon juice and rind, garlic and fresh herbs, then season with salt and pepper. Pour a little of the mixture over each fillet, bring up the edges and seal.

STEP 5

Bake for 10 minutes or until fish is cooked through - it will flake away easily when tested with a fork. Drizzle with remaining dressing, and serve with boiled chat potatoes, if desired.

NUTRITION VALUE

1735 KJ Energy, 20g fat, 3g saturated fat, 3g fiber, 21g protein, 3g carbs.

KINGFISH SKEWERS WITH CHARGRILLED TOMATOES AND CHILLIES

These gluten-free kingfish skewers make a light and lovely lunch.

MAKES 4 SERVING/ TOTAL TIME 35 MINUTE

INGREDIENTS

1/4 cup (60ml) lemon juice

5-6 parsley sprigs, leaves roughly chopped

1/2 teaspoon dried chili flakes

1 1/2 tablespoons olive oil

800g skinless kingfish fillets, pin boned, cut into 3cm cubes

3 long red chilies

3 long green chilies

250g vine-ripened cherry tomatoes

METHOD

STEP 1

Soak 8 wooden skewers in water for 10 minutes. Combine juice, parsley, dried chili, 2 teaspoons oil and fish in a bowl. Cover and refrigerate for 10 minutes, then thread onto skewers.

STEP 2

Meanwhile, toss chilies and tomatoes in remaining olive oil. Heat an oiled chargrill or barbecue over medium-high heat. When hot, cook chilies for 10 minutes, turning to blacken. The skin should pop and crack open. Cut open each chili down one side and remove seeds (unless you like it really spicy).

STEP 3

Add the kingfish skewers to the chargrill or barbecue and cook for 6-8 minutes, turning once, or until just cooked. Add the tomatoes and cook for the final 5 minutes, or until softened and lightly charred.

Serve 2 skewers per person with chargrilled tomatoes and chilies.

NUTRITION VALUE	1240 KJ Energy, 11.7g fat, 2.6g saturated fat, 2.4g fiber, 42.6g protein, 3.1g carbs.

CHICKEN WITH LEMON AND GARLIC

Lemon and garlic add flavor to the chicken as well as ensuring it is extra juicy.

MAKES 4 SERVING/ TOTAL TIME 35 MINUTE

INGREDIENTS

4 **chicken Maryland** pieces

2 teaspoons thyme leaves

1 tablespoon finely grated lemon rind

2 cloves garlic, crushed

85g unsalted butter, softened

METHOD

STEP 1

Pre-heat oven to 220°C. Place the lemon rind, butter, garlic, thyme leaves, salt and pepper in a bowl and mix until combined. Set aside.

STEP 2

Using your fingers or the back of a teaspoon, push deeply but gently between the skin and flesh of each chicken Maryland piece to separate them and form a pocket. Divide the lemon butter mixture between four chicken thighs, pushing the butter evenly down towards the drumstick. Wipe any remaining butter over the surface of the chicken skin.

STEP 3

Place the chicken in a large baking dish lined with baking paper. Scatter a few extra thyme sprigs in the dish. Bake for 25 minutes, basting regularly until golden. Serve with steamed vegetables.

NUTRITION VALUE

1617 KJ Energy, 20g fat, 1g fiber, 35g protein, 14.9g carbs.

INSTANT POT BRISKET TACO BOWLS

Briny brisket all seasoned up, then shredded to crispy perfection. Nuzzled up to some spiced cauliflower rice, shredded lettuce and avocado.

MAKES 3 SERVING/ TOTAL TIME 1 HOUR 17 MINUTE

INGREDIENTS

2 pound brisket

2 teaspoons fine salt

2 tablespoons mustard seeds

2 bay leaves

1 teaspoon nutmeg

1 tablespoon cumin

1 tablespoon garlic powder

2 tablespoons grated beetroot

3 tablespoons vinegar

3 cups bone broth plus water

16 ounces cauliflower rice

2 tablespoons avocado oil

1 teaspoon turmeric

1 teaspoon garlic salt

1 teaspoon dried oregano

METHOD

STEP 1

Combine the brisket seasonings and rub into the meat. Add the beetroot and vinegar. Toss and set to marinate in the fridge for 30 minutes. When ready to cook, heat the pressure cooker on sauté mode. When hot, add the brisket, fatty side down and sear for 2 minutes, then flip and sear the other side. Cancel the sauce function. Add in the bone broth, then enough water to submerge the brisket. Pour in any leftover marinade. Set to pressure cook on high for 50 minutes. Release the pressure manually. Remove the brisket from the pressure cooker and set it on a sheet pan. Shred with two forks.

STEP 2

Place the oven rack right under the broiler. Heat the broiler at 500F.

Spread the brisket out over half of the sheet pan and spoon a little liquid from the pressure cooker over it. On the other half of the sheet pan toss the cauliflower rice with avocado oil and seasoning and spread out flat on the sheet pan. To make your bowls, distribute the cauliflower rice and brisket. Add shredded lettuce, avocado, cilantro and green onion.

NUTRITION VALUE

806 Kcal, 20g fat,
10g fiber, 79g protein, 14g carbs.

PALEO JAMBALAYA

The following recipe will set you out on a hunt for the best andouille sausages you can find.

MAKES 4 SERVING/ TOTAL TIME 35 MINUTE

INGREDIENTS

2 tbsp. olive oil

1 lb. Andouille sausages, sliced

2 lbs. chicken tenders,

1 onion, chopped3 cloves garlic, minced

3 celery stalks, chopped

1 green bell pepper, sliced

1 red bell pepper, sliced

4 fresh thyme sprigs

2 cups chicken broth

1 cup tomato sauce

1/4 cup hot sauce (optional)

1 lb. raw shrimp,

8 oz. okra, chopped

2 tbsp. parsley, finely chopped

4 green onions, chopped

METHOD

STEP 1

In a large saucepan over high heat, brown the sausages in the olive oil. Cook for approximately 3 minutes, or until golden brown.

Add the chicken to the saucepan and season with salt and pepper. Continue cooking on all sides for a few more minutes until the chicken begins to brown.

STEP 2

Add the onion, garlic, celery, peppers and thyme to the saucepan. Mix in with the meat and continue to cook for 5 to 7 minutes; stirring frequently to prevent anything from sticking to the bottom of the pan.

Add the broth, tomato sauce and hot sauce. Mix well and allow it to come to a boil.

Once the mixture has boiled, add the shrimp and okra. Reduce the heat and simmer, covered, for 5 to 7 minutes, or until shrimp is pink.

Remove the jambalaya from the heat. Stir in parsley and green onions prior to serving.

NUTRITION VALUE

800 Kcal, 20g fat, 57g protein, 13g carbs.

CHICKEN WITH SPINACH, SWEET POTATOES AND MUSHROOMS

Chicken often makes a delightful appearance with mashed sweet potatoes and green vegetables.

MAKES 4 SERVING/ TOTAL TIME 60 MINUTE

INGREDIENTS

2 lbs. chicken breasts, skinless, boneless and sliced

2 sweet potatoes, peeled and diced

10 mushrooms, sliced

1 red onion, sliced

2 garlic cloves, minced

2 cups baby spinach

1/2 cup chicken stock

1 cup coconut milk

1 tbsp. garlic powder

1 tbsp. onion powder

1 tbsp. paprika

1 tbsp. coconut oil

METHOD

STEP 1

Preheat oven to 375 F. In a bowl, combine the garlic powder, onion powder and paprika, then season to taste. Season the chicken pieces with the spice mixture. Melt the coconut oil in a skillet over medium-high heat. Brown the chicken in the skillet on both sides, 2 to 3 minutes per side; then transfer to a baking dish. Cook the diced sweet potatoes for 5 to 6 minutes in the skillet over medium heat. Add more coconut oil if needed.

STEP 2

Add the onion, mushrooms, and garlic to the sweet potatoes and cook for another 2 to 3 minutes. Add the sweet potatoes, onion, mushrooms, and garlic to the baking dish. Pour in the coconut milk and chicken stock. Top with baby spinach, give everything a toss. Place in the oven and bake for 18 to 20 minutes, covered. Bake another 10 minutes uncovered.

NUTRITION VALUE

20g fat, 74g protein, 15g carbs.

CURRIED MANGO SHRIMP KEBOBS

Sweet and spicy, these easy kebobs will be the hit of your next backyard barbecue. Make them up in advance and then grill when ready to eat.

MAKES 4 SERVING/ TOTAL TIME 20 MINUTE

INGREDIENTS

1 pound raw shrimp

2 cups diced mango

1 tablespoon melted coconut oil

1 teaspoon curry powder

METHOD

STEP 1

Thread the shrimp and mango onto skewers. Brush with coconut oil and sprinkle with curry powder.

STEP 2

Preheat a gas or charcoal grill to medium high heat. Grill until shrimp is pink and mango is lightly charred. Serve

NUTRITION VALUE

162 Kcal, 5g fat,
2g fiber, 20g protein, 14g carbs.

BACON MUSHROOM THYME BURGERS

Loaded with salty bacon and mushrooms, these burgers are so delicious, you won't miss the bun!

MAKES 4 SERVING/ TOTAL TIME 20 MINUTE

INGREDIENTS

1 pound ground beef

1 egg

1 cup finely chopped mushrooms

1 teaspoon fresh thyme leaves

4 slices bacon cooked and crumbled

Sea salt and fresh ground pepper to taste

METHOD

STEP 1

Combine the beef, egg, mushroom, thyme and bacon with a pinch of salt and pepper. Form into 4 patties.

STEP 2

Preheat a gas or charcoal grill to medium heat. Grill the burgers until done to your liking and serve with your favorite toppings.

NUTRITION VALUE

266Kcal, 17g fat,
28g protein, 1g carbs.

DIJON HERB CHICKEN SALAD

Lots of herbs and a garlic mustard dressing turn traditional chicken salad into a new, exciting dish. It's creamy, flavorful, and delicious, while still being nutritious and filling — a win when it comes to lunch!

MAKES 2 SERVING/ TOTAL TIME 15 MINUTE

INGREDIENTS

1/4 cup plain Greek yogurt

1 tablespoon Dijon mustard

2 cloves garlic minced

1 teaspoon apple cider vinegar

2 tablespoons chopped fresh parsley

1 tablespoon chopped thyme leaves

1 tablespoon chopped rosemary leaves

2 cups cooked and shredded chicken breast

1 red onion sliced

Lettuce leaves or spinach for serving

Sea salt and fresh ground pepper to taste

METHOD

STEP 1

Whisk the yogurt, mustard, garlic, and cider vinegar in a bowl. Add the remaining ingredients and mix well.

Chill until ready to serve.

Serve in the lettuce leaves or over a bed of spinach.

NUTRITION VALUE

459 Kcal, 10g fat,
3g fiber, 73g protein, 14.9g carbs.

PESTO SHRIMP SALAD

This easy shrimp salad comes together quickly and tastes amazing. Perfect for a quick lunch that is high in protein and flavor.

MAKES 1 SERVING/ TOTAL TIME 10 MINUTE

INGREDIENTS

1/2 cup basil leaves

1 clove garlic

2 tablespoons chopped walnuts

Juice of 1 lemon

1/4 cup olive oil

2 5- ounce cans cooked shrimp drained

1 cup halved cherry tomatoes

1 small red onion sliced

2 cups arugula

Sea salt and fresh ground pepper to taste

METHOD

STEP 1

Put the basil, garlic, walnuts, lemon juice, and olive oil in blender or food processor and blend until smooth. Toss the pesto with the remaining ingredients, and chill until ready to serve.

NUTRITION VALUE

410 Kcal, 20g fat,
4g fiber, 26g protein, 11g carbs.

BALSAMIC GRILLED PORK TENDERLOIN

Instead of grilling the same chicken breast or burgers, try your hand at this easy balsamic pork tenderloin. It's juicy and flavorful, and perfect with your favorite vegetable or salad.

MAKES 4 SERVING/ TOTAL TIME 40 MINUTE

INGREDIENTS

1/2 cup balsamic vinegar

2 tablespoons honey

1 teaspoon crushed red pepper flakes

1/2 teaspoon sea salt

1/2 teaspoon black pepper

1 pork tenderloin

METHOD

STEP 1

Put all of the ingredients in a freezer bag and mix well, covering the pork. Marinate in the refrigerator for 1-2 hours.

STEP 2

When ready to cook, preheat grill to medium high heat. Grill the pork until internal temperature reaches 165 degrees F. Let rest for 10-15 minutes before slicing. Serve with your favorite vegetables on the side.

NUTRITION VALUE

353 Kcal, 10g fat, 58g protein, 14g carbs.

TUNA CAKES WITH LEMON PARSLEY SLAW

Turn a can of tuna into an easy and nutritious meal with this easy recipe. It's perfect for a quick lunch or dinner, and makes a filling meal you can count on.

MAKES 2 SERVING/ TOTAL TIME 20 MINUTE

INGREDIENTS

Lemon Parsley Slaw:

2 tablespoons olive oil based mayonnaise

Juice and zest of 1/2 lemon

1 clove garlic minced

2 tablespoons finely chopped parsley

2 cups finely shredded cabbage

Sea salt and fresh ground pepper to taste

Tuna Cakes:

2 5- ounce cans tuna drained

4 green onions sliced

1 clove garlic minced

Juice and zest of 1/2 lemon

1/2 cup almond flour

1/2 teaspoon sea salt

2 eggs

METHOD

STEP 1

Make the slaw by whisking the mayo, lemon, and garlic in a large bowl. Add the cabbage and parsley, season with salt and pepper. Stir and set aside.

STEP 2

To make the tuna cakes, mix the tuna, green onions, garlic, lemon, almond flour, salt and eggs in a large bowl. Mix well and form into 4 patties.

Heat a skillet over medium high heat and add the oil. Fry the tuna cakes until browned on both sides. Serve over the slaw.

NUTRITION VALUE	351 Kcal, 20g fat, 5g fiber, 22g protein, 10g carbs.

COCONUT SHRIMP WITH MANGO SLAW

A sweet and savory salad is served with crispy coconut shrimp for a meal that is nutritious, filling, and satisfying.

MAKES 2 SERVING/ TOTAL TIME 20 MINUTE

INGREDIENTS

2 cups finely shredded cabbage

1 jalapeno minced

1 mango diced

1/2 cup chopped cilantro

Juice of 1 lime

1/2 cup unsweetened shredded coconut

1/2 cup almond flour

1/2 teaspoon garlic powder

1/4 teaspoon cayenne pepper

1 pound peeled and deveined shrimp

1 egg

METHOD

STEP 1

Preheat oven to 400 degrees F.

Combine the cabbage, jalapeno, mango cilantro, and lime juice in a large bowl and toss. Set aside.

In a wide, shallow dish, combine the coconut, almond flour, garlic, and cayenne. In a separate bowl, beat the egg.

STEP 2

Dip the shrimp in the egg, followed by the coconut mixture. Lay the shrimp on a parchment lined baking sheet.

Bake for 8-10 minutes, until the shrimp is golden brown and cook through.

Serve with the slaw.

NUTRITION VALUE

469 Kcal, 19g fat,
8g fiber, 45g protein, 15g carbs.

LEMON CAPER CHICKEN AND GARLIC SPINACH

Capers add a ton of flavor to this dish without any bad stuff, and when paired with garlicky spinach, this becomes an amazing meal.

MAKES 2 SERVING/ TOTAL TIME 30 MINUTE

INGREDIENTS

2 chicken breasts

2 tablespoons olive oil

Juice of 1 lemon

2 tablespoons capers

2 cloves garlic minced

6 cups baby spinach

Sea salt and fresh ground pepper to taste

METHOD

STEP 1

Using a meat mallet, pound the chicken breasts until they are an even thickness. Season with salt and pepper.

Heat half the oil over medium high heat in a heavy skillet and add the chicken. Cook until chicken easily releases from the pan with a spatula and flip. Add the lemon juice and capers to the pan.

STEP 2

Cover and cook on low for 5 minutes.

Remove chicken from the pan, and add the remaining oil. Add the garlic and sauté for 30 seconds. Add the spinach to the pan as quickly as you can and cook until wilted.

Serve the spinach with the chicken.

NUTRITION VALUE	256 Kcal, 15g fat, 3g fiber, 23g protein, 8g carbs.

CASHEW ORANGE CHICKEN

For the perfect combination of sweet and salty, this dish has it all — healthy protein, heart healthy fats, and lots of vitamins and minerals.

MAKES 4 SERVING/ TOTAL TIME 45 MINUTE

INGREDIENTS

2 cup pineapple juice

Juice and zest of 2 oranges

2 tablespoons coconut sugar

1 tablespoon Paleo fish sauce

1 1/2 pounds chicken breast cut into bite sized pieces

1/2 cup almond flour

4 cups cauliflower rice

4 green onions sliced

1/2 cup roasted cashews

Sea salt and fresh ground pepper to taste

METHOD

STEP 1

Preheat oven to 400 degrees F. Line a baking sheet with parchment paper or foil.

Put the pineapple juice, orange juice and zest, coconut sugar, and fish sauce in a large saucepan. Bring to a boil and reduce to a low simmer. Simmer for 15 minutes, until reduced to a thick syrup. Remove from heat. Add the chicken pieces and coat well.

STEP 2

Dredge the coated chicken pieces with the almond flour and transfer to baking sheet. Bake for 10-15 minutes, until chicken is cooked through.

While the chicken is baking, steam the cauliflower rice with the green onions until tender and then stir in the cashews.

Top the cauliflower rice with the chicken and serve.

NUTRITION VALUE

410 Kcal, 12g fat, 3g fiber, 20g protein, 14g carbs.

EGG SALAD STUFFED AVOCADO

Healthy protein and high quality fats make the perfect lunch. It's also super portable — pack your egg salad and avocado and then assemble right when you're ready to eat.

MAKES 1 SERVING/ TOTAL TIME 15 MINUTE

INGREDIENTS

2 hard boiled eggs

1 tablespoon Paleo mayonnaise

1 tablespoon relish

1 teaspoon Dijon mustard

1 avocado

Sea salt and fresh ground pepper to taste

METHOD

STEP 1

Rough chop the eggs and add to a bowl with the relish, mayo, and mustard.

STEP 2

Cut the avocado in half and remove the pit. Scoop half the flesh out of each side and add to the bowl with the eggs.

Mash well, and season with salt and pepper.

Spoon into the avocado shells and serve.

NUTRITION VALUE

480 Kcal, 20g fat,
10g fiber, 20g protein, 14g carbs.

SALMON KALE SALAD

Pan seared salmon is extra crispy and delicious and adds flavor and protein to this quick and easy salad.

MAKES 2 SERVING/ TOTAL TIME 20 MINUTE

INGREDIENTS

1/4 cup olive oil plus 1 tablespoon

Juice of 1 lemon

1 clove garlic minced

1 shallot minced

1 teaspoon Dijon mustard

1 bunch of kale shredded

1 cup cherry tomatoes halved

1 small cucumber diced

4 slices cooked and crumbled bacon

2 salmon filets

Sea salt and fresh ground pepper to taste

METHOD

STEP 1

Put 1/4 cup olive oil, lemon juice, garlic, shallot, and mustard in a large bowl. Whisk until well combined. Add the kale, tomatoes, and bacon and toss.

STEP 2

Heat the remaining tablespoon of oil in a heavy skillet. Season the salmon filets with salt and pepper and add to the pan. Cook until golden brown and done to your liking.

Serve on top of the salad.

NUTRITION VALUE	531 Kcal, 30g fat, 6g fiber, 29g protein, 15g carbs.

STEAK BURRITO BOWLS

Recipe that Everyone love.

MAKES 2 SERVING/ TOTAL TIME 20 MINUTE

INGREDIENTS

1 tablespoon olive oil

1/2 pound sirloin steak cut into strips

1 bell pepper sliced

1 onion sliced

1 jalapeno sliced

1 teaspoon chili powder

1 teaspoon cumin

1 teaspoon garlic powder

2 cups riced cauliflower

1/2 cup finely chopped cilantro

Juice of 1 lime

To serve: guacamole salsa, shredded lettuce, hot sauce

METHOD

STEP 1

Preheat oven to 450 degrees Toss the oil with the steak, peppers, onions, and seasonings. Lay on a sheet pan and bake for 10-12 minutes, until steak is done and veggies are lightly caramelized. Remove from oven.

STEP 2

Combine the rice, cilantro, and lime juice in a bowl and steam in the microwave until cauliflower is tender. Season with salt and pepper.
Serve the rice, steak and veggies in a bowl topped with guacamole, salsa, and lettuce.

NUTRITION VALUE

335 Kcal, 14g fat,
8g fiber, 32g protein, 15g carbs.

SHEET PAN CHICKEN FAJITAS

All you have to do is cut your meat up into thin even strips. Cut your veggies up the same way. Throw it all on a pan with some spices and cook for about 15 minutes .

MAKES 4 SERVING/ TOTAL TIME 45 MINUTE

INGREDIENTS

1.5 pound chicken breast cut into strips

3 bell peppers any color, cut into strips

1 red onion sliced

1 cup sliced mushrooms

1 tsp chili powder

.5 tsp cumin

.5 tsp garlic powder

.5 tsp onion powder

.5 tsp dried oregano

.5 tsp sea salt

.5 cup finely chopped cilantro

juice of 1 lime

large, crisp lettuce leaves

guacamole and salsa for serving

METHOD
STEP 1

Preheat oven to 450 degrees F.
Toss the meat, peppers, onions, and mushrooms with the seasonings. Roast for 10-15 minutes until chicken is done and veggies are browned.

STEP 2
Remove from oven, sprinkle with cilantro and lime juice.
Serve in the lettuce leaves topped with your desired toppings.

NUTRITION VALUE

335 Kcal, 14g fat,
8g fiber, 32g protein, 15g carbs.

CURRIED CHICKEN STEW

Recipe that Everyone love.

MAKES 4 SERVING/ TOTAL TIME 30 MINUTE

INGREDIENTS

4 tablespoons coconut oil

1 onion diced

2 cloves garlic minced

1 teaspoon grated ginger

1 teaspoon curry powder

4 cups chopped greens such as kale or chard

1 pound chicken breast

2 cups chicken broth

1 cup coconut milk

2 cups riced cauliflower

To serve: hot sauce shredded coconut, lime wedges

Sea salt and fresh ground pepper to taste

METHOD

STEP 1

Heat the oil in a large pot or Dutch oven to medium high heat. Add the onion, garlic, and ginger, and cook until softened. Stir in the curry powder and greens and cook until greens are softened. Add the curry powder, chicken breast, and broth. Bring to a boil and reduce to a simmer.

STEP 2

Simmer until chicken is cooked through. Remove breasts from pot and shred with two forks. Return to the pot and add the coconut milk and cauliflower. Simmer for 5 minutes. Serve immediately.

NUTRITION VALUE

435 Kcal, 20g fat,
3.3g fiber, 29.5g protein, 10.1g carbs.

LEMON CAPER TUNA WRAPS

se easy lettuce wraps require pretty much that same amount of effort as opening a can of tuna, but they are loaded with flavor, thanks in part to caper berries, tiny round berries that are pickled to be salty and briny. Perfect with tuna.

MAKES 1 SERVING/ TOTAL TIME 10 MINUTE

INGREDIENTS

1 5 oz can of tuna drained

1 tablespoons olive oil

Juice and zest of 1 lemon

1 tablespoon capers

1 tablespoon fresh chopped parsley

1 clove garlic minced

2 firm crisp lettuce leaves left intact

1/4 cup diced tomatoes

Sea salt and fresh ground pepper to taste

METHOD

STEP 1
Combine the tuna, oil, lemon , capers, parsley and garlic in a bowl. Season with salt and pepper. Spoon into the lettuce leaves and top with the tomatoes before serving.

NUTRITION VALUE

467 Kcal, 20g fat,
1g fiber, 48.1g protein, 3.4g carbs.

CAULIFLOWER RICE STEAK BOWL

A quick and easy bowl filled with tender beef, caramelized Brussels sprouts and cauliflower rice makes the perfect healthy lunch option.

MAKES 2 SERVING/ TOTAL TIME 20 MINUTE

INGREDIENTS

3 tablespoons olive oil

10 ounces sirloin steak cubed

1 pound Brussels sprouts cored and halved

2 cups riced cauliflower

Juice of 1 lemon

1/4 cup sliced almonds

Sea salt and fresh ground pepper to taste

METHOD

STEP 1

Heat the oil in a heavy skillet over medium heat. Add the steak and cook until well browned. Remove from pan, leaving as much of the fat behind as possible. Add the Brussels sprouts cut side down and sear until well browned.

STEP 2

Flip and continue cooking for another minute or two. Add the cauliflower and cook until softened. Add the lemon juice, almonds, and steak and cook until heated through. Serve immediately.

NUTRITION VALUE

625 Kcal, 20 fat,
11g fiber, 54.2g protein, 14 carbs.

JUICY ITALIAN CHICKEN BREAST

Take the guesswork out of chicken breasts with this easy, fast recipe. Serve these with your favorite veggies or slice and add to a big green salad for a healthy meal in a flash.

MAKES 4 SERVING/ TOTAL TIME 10 MINUTE

INGREDIENTS

4 6-ounce chicken breasts

1 teaspoon Italian seasoning

2 tablespoons olive oil

1 cup chicken broth or water

Juice of 1 lemon

Sea salt and fresh ground pepper to taste

METHOD

STEP 1

Season your chicken with the Italian seasoning and salt and pepper. Using the sauté setting on your Instant Pot, add the oil and the chicken breasts, and cook for about 2 minutes per side. Remove from the pot and add the broth or water to the bottom.

STEP 2

Set the steamer rack in the pot and add the chicken to the rack. Drizzle with the lemon juice.

Close your pot and set your timer to 5 minutes at high pressure.

Remove the chicken and allow to rest for a few minutes before serving.

NUTRITION VALUE

467 Kcal, 20g fat,
1g fiber, 48.1g protein, 3.4g carbs.

LEMON CHICKEN BRUSSELS SPROUT SALAD

When paired with chicken, bacon, and a tangy lemon dressing, it turns lunch time into something you'll look forward to.

MAKES 4 SERVING/ TOTAL TIME 20 MINUTE

INGREDIENTS

4 slices bacon chopped

1 pound chicken breasts

1 pound Brussels sprouts cored and finely shredded

1/2 cup olive oil

Juice and zest of 1 lemon

1 teaspoon Dijon mustard

1 clove garlic minced

Sea salt and fresh ground pepper to taste

METHOD

STEP 1

Heat a skillet to medium heat and cook the bacon pieces until crisp. Remove with a slotted spoon, leaving the fat behind. Add the chicken and cook until browned and cooked through. Remove the chicken from the pan and let cool, then shred with two forks.

STEP 2

Put the sprouts in a bowl with the bacon. Add the chicken. Put the remaining ingredients in a jar and shake until well combined. Toss with the salad and serve.

NUTRITION VALUE

544 Kcal, 20g fat, 0.8g fiber, 40.6g protein, 2.3g carbs.

LEMON DILL SALMON

Serve it with steamed veggies and a salad for complete healthy meal.

MAKES 2 SERVING/ TOTAL TIME 20 MINUTE

INGREDIENTS

2 salmon filets

3 tablespoons olive oil

1 tablespoon finely chopped fresh dill

1/2 lemon sliced

Sea salt and fresh ground pepper to taste

METHOD

STEP 1

Preheat oven to 375 degrees F.

Put the salmon filets on a baking sheet and season with salt and pepper. Brush with olive oil, sprinkle with dill, and lay a few lemon slices over each piece.

Bake for 10-15 minutes, until salmon is cooked to your liking, and serve.

NUTRITION VALUE

334 Kcal, 20g fat,
0.2g fiber, 36.3g protein, 0.9g carbs.

PAN SEARED SCALLOPS WITH CAULIFLOWER RICE

Scallops are something many people only eat in restaurants, and they pay a pretty penny for them. Fortunately, they are surprisingly easy (and fast!) to cook, making an elegant, succulent restaurant meal totally doable at home.

MAKES 2 SERVING/ TOTAL TIME 20 MINUTE

INGREDIENTS

2 tablespoons olive oil divided

2 cloves garlic minced

2 cups finely chopped cauliflower

12 ounces sea scallops dried with paper towels

1 lemon juiced

Sea salt and fresh ground pepper to taste

METHOD

STEP 1

Heat half the oil in a heavy skillet. Add the garlic and cook for 1 minute. Add the cauliflower and cook until browned and softened. Remove from pan and add the remaining oil.

STEP 2

Season the scallops liberally with salt and pepper and add to the pan. Cook for about 2 minutes per side, until well browned, being careful not to overcook. Drizzle with the lemon juice.
Serve over the cauliflower rice.

NUTRITION VALUE

197 Kcal, 13g fat,
5.8g fiber, 10g protein, 14.8g carbs.

SLOW COOKED MUSHROOMS

Mushrooms take on new life when slow cooked in olive oil and herbs. Use these to top steaks, add to salads, or even enjoy as a side.

MAKES 1 SERVING/ TOTAL TIME 2 HOUR

INGREDIENTS

2 cups sliced mushrooms

2 sprigs thyme

2 cloves garlic smashed

1/4 cup olive oil

1/2 cup chicken broth

1/2 teaspoon sea salt

METHOD

STEP 1
Put all ingredients in a slow cooker and cook over low heat for 2 hours. Serve immediately, or cool and store in the refrigerator until ready to serve.

NUTRITION VALUE

62 Kcal, 4g fat,
1g fiber, 4g protein, 2g carbs.

HOT PEPPER HONEY GLAZED CHICKEN THIGHS

Sweet, spicy, and rich with flavor, these chicken thighs are the perfect weeknight meal. Serve with sautéed spinach or mashed cauliflower for a complete meal.

MAKES 2 SERVING/ TOTAL TIME 40 MINUTE

INGREDIENTS

2 tablespoons sesame oil

1 teaspoon ground ginger

2 green onions sliced

1 clove garlic minced

1 teaspoon crushed red pepper flakes

12 ounces chicken thighs

1 cup chicken broth

1/4 cup honey

Sea salt and fresh ground pepper to taste

METHOD

STEP 1

Preheat oven to 375 degrees F. Line a baking sheet with foil or parchment.

Heat the oil in a heavy bottomed skillet. Add the ginger, green onions, garlic, and pepper flakes. Cook for about a minute and add the chicken to the pan.

Cook the chicken until browned on both sides and transfer to the prepared baking sheet, leaving the remaining ingredients in the pan. Bake for 25-35 minutes, until chicken is cooked through.

STEP 2

While the chicken is in the oven, add the broth and honey to the pan the chicken was cooked in. Bring to a rolling boil, reduce to a simmer, and simmer until reduced by about half.

When the chicken is done, serve it drizzled with the honey glaze.

NUTRITION VALUE

531 Kcal, 30g fat, 6g fiber, 29g protein, 15g carbs.

AIR FRYER CHICKEN WINGS

A super simple way to cook chicken wings in the air fryer. Plus a classic Buffalo wings sauce with just 2 ingredients.

MAKES 3 SERVING/ TOTAL TIME 35 MINUTE

INGREDIENTS

1-½ pounds chicken wings (about 12 pieces)

Buffalo Wing Sauce

¼ cup ghee or butter-flavored coconut oil

¼ cup hot sauce

For Serving

celery sticks

ranch dip

METHOD

STEP 1

Cut wings apart, if needed, using a heavy knife to cut at joints. Place wings in the air fryer basket leaving a little room in between so they can get crispy. Add a second layer using a rack inserted in the basket if desired. Cook at 390 degrees for 15 - 20 minutes. Turn wings over and cook 10 - 15 minutes longer until the skin is golden brown and crisp. Place wings in a large bowl to toss with sauce.

STEP 2

To make the sauce

Melt the ghee and whisk with hot sauce. Drizzle some of the sauce over wings and toss. Serve immediately with remaining sauce, celery sticks and ranch dip on the side.

NUTRITION VALUE	405 Cal, 20g fat, 23g protein, 1g carbs.

ITALIAN BRAISED GREENS

These hearty greens get tons of flavor from crisp bacon, and are loaded with nutrients. Use sturdy greens like collards orchard that will hold up nicely to a braise.

MAKES 4 SERVING/ TOTAL TIME 20 MINUTE

INGREDIENTS

4 slices bacon chopped

2 cloves garlic minced

6 cups hearty winter greens such as chard kale, or mustard greens

1/2 cup chicken broth

Juice of 1 lemon

Sea salt and fresh ground pepper to taste

METHOD
STEP 1

Cook the bacon in a heavy straight-sided skillet. Remove with a slotted spoon and set aside.

Add the garlic and the greens to the pan and sauté for a minute or two. Add the broth, and bring to a low simmer.

STEP 2

Braise for 10 minutes, until greens are tender and liquid is reduced. Stir in the lemon juice and turn off heat. Stir in the reserved bacon and serve.

NUTRITION VALUE

353 Kcal, 15g fat,
8g fiber, 35g protein, 15g carbs.

MEDITERRANEAN STUFFED CHICKEN BREASTS

These delicious stuffed chicken breasts will seem like something complicated and time consuming, but in reality, couldn't be simpler. Serve with cauliflower rice or your favorite

MAKES 4 SERVING/ TOTAL TIME 8 HOUR

INGREDIENTS

1/4 cup chopped kalamata olives

1/4 cup chopped sundried tomatoes

1 tablespoon fresh chopped parsley

1/2 tablespoon fresh chopped oregano

2 green onions minced

1/2 teaspoon sea salt

4 thick chicken breasts

2 tablespoons olive oil

1 cup chicken broth

METHOD
STEP 1

Combine the olives, tomatoes, parsley, oregano, green onions, and salt in a bowl and mix well.
Carefully cut a slit into the thickest part of each chicken breast, being careful not to slice all the way through. Fill each with the olive mixture.

STEP 2

Lay the chicken breasts in your crockpot and brush with the oil. Cover with the broth and cook on low heat for 6-8 hours, until cooked through.

NUTRITION VALUE

531 Kcal, 30g fat,
6g fiber, 29g protein, 15g carbs.

VEGGIE FRITTERS WITH CHIVE COCONUT CREAM

These quick and easy veggie fritters are crispy and flavorful. They make a nice side for grilled meats.

MAKES 4 SERVING/ TOTAL TIME 20 MINUTE

INGREDIENTS

Fritters:

1 summer squash shredded

1 zucchini shredded

1 carrot shredded

1/2 cup finely shredded cabbage

1 egg

1/2 cup almond flour

1/2 cup coconut milk

1/2 teaspoon sea salt

2 tablespoons olive oil

Chive Coconut Cream:

1/2 cup coconut cream

1/2 teaspoon sea salt

1 teaspoon minced chives

METHOD

STEP 1

Combine all of the ingredients for the fritters except the oil in a large bowl and mix well.

Heat the oil in heavy bottomed skillet. Drop the veggie mixture by large spoonfuls into the hot oil and fry until golden on both sides.

STEP 2

To make the coconut cream, whisk the cream, salt, and chives in a small bowl. Serve with the fritters.

NUTRITION VALUE

358 Kcal, 20g fat, 4.5g fiber, 26.1g protein, 11.6g carbs.

BISON POT ROAST

Pot roast is the dish your slow cooker is made for, and when you take one bite of this melt in your mouth bison, you'll understand why. This is so simple, yet so delicious.

MAKES 2 SERVING/ TOTAL TIME 9 HOUR

INGREDIENTS

1 2- pound bison roast

2 cups baby carrots

1 large onion sliced

4 cloves garlic smashed

2 bay leaves

2 tablespoons cider vinegar

2 cups chicken or beef broth more or less to cover roast

Sea salt and fresh ground pepper to taste

METHOD
STEP 1

Put all of the ingredients in your slow cooker pot and cover.

Turn on low heat and cook for at least 8 hours, or until meat is tender and falls apart easily.

NUTRITION VALUE

241 Kcal, 20g fat,
13.6g fiber, 21g protein, 11g carbs.

PORK AND NOODLES

Pork tenderloin is tender and juicy, and pairs perfectly with zucchini noodles for a healthy, guilt-free meal.

MAKES 4 SERVING/ TOTAL TIME 20 MINUTE

INGREDIENTS

2 tablespoons sesame oil

1 teaspoon grated ginger

2 garlic cloves minced

1/2 onion diced

1 1 1/2 pound pork loin

8 ounces baby carrots

1 cup chicken broth

1 tablespoon apple cider vinegar

1 teaspoon sea salt

2 large zucchini cut into noodles

METHOD
STEP 1

Using the sauté setting on your Instant Pot, heat the sesame oil, and add the ginger, garlic, and onions. Cook for 5 minutes, until translucent.

STEP 2

Add the remaining ingredients, except for the zucchini noodles, and close the pot lid. Set to cook for 15 minutes at high pressure.
Remove the lid, add the noodles, and stir. Cover for 5 minutes, until noodles are tender, and serve.

NUTRITION VALUE

253 Kcal, 10g fat,
7g fiber, 46g protein, 15g carbs.

PAN SEARED CHICKEN WITH CAULIFLOWER CREAM SAUCE

Succulent browned chicken gets a healthy, delicious boost of flavor from cauliflower cream sauce. It's rich, delicious, and comforting and the perfect meal after a long day.

MAKES 4 SERVING/ TOTAL TIME 20 MINUTE

INGREDIENTS

Cauliflower Cream Sauce:

2 tablespoons olive oil

3 cloves garlic minced

2 cups finely chopped cauliflower

1 cup chicken broth more or less depending on consistency

1/2 teaspoon sea salt

1/4 cup unsweetened almond milk

1 tablespoon lemon juice

Pan Seared Chicken:

4 chicken breasts pounded to an even thickness

2 tablespoons olive oil

Sea salt and black pepper to taste

METHOD
STEP 1

To make the sauce, heat the oil and add the garlic and cauliflower. Stir and cook until cauliflower is lightly browned and very soft. Transfer to a blender and add the salt. Puree, adding the broth a little bit at a time until you get a good consistency. Stir in the milk and lemon juice.

STEP 2

To cook the chicken, season liberally with salt and pepper. Heat the oil in a heavy skillet and add the chicken breasts, making sure not to crowd the pan.

Cook the chicken until browned on both sides, and cooked through.

Serve the chicken topped with the sauce, alongside your favorite veggies or Paleo sides.

NUTRITION VALUE	335 Kcal, 14g fat, 8g fiber, 32g protein, 15g carbs.

SWEET AND SOUR CABBAGE

Your Instant Pot is perfect for getting your sides on the table while you're working on your main dish, and this super easy cabbage recipe is great for pork or beef. Use a coleslaw mix to make it quicker and easier, and also add color and flavor.

MAKES 4 SERVING/ TOTAL TIME 15 MINUTE

INGREDIENTS

2 tablespoons olive oil

1 small onion sliced

2 cloves garlic minced

1 apple shredded

6 cups shredded cabbage any color

1 cup chicken broth

1 tablespoon apple cider vinegar

Sea salt and fresh ground pepper to taste

METHOD

STEP 1

Using the sauté setting on your Instant Pot, heat the oil and cook the onions, garlic, and apple until translucent. Add the remaining ingredients, and cook on high pressure for 10 minutes.

NUTRITION VALUE

480Kcal, 17g fat, 19g fiber, 20g protein, 14.6g carbs.

SLOW COOKER PAPRIKA CHICKEN

This easy and flavorful chicken dish requires absolutely no effort, but promises big flavor. For extra flair, use a combination of sweet and smoked paprika.

MAKES 4 SERVING/ TOTAL TIME 8 HOUR

INGREDIENTS

1 1/2 pounds bone-in chicken pieces

1 onion sliced

1 tablespoon paprika

1 tablespoon lemon juice

2 cups chicken broth

Sea salt and fresh ground pepper to taste

METHOD

STEP 1
Put all of the ingredients in your slow cooker pot and cover.

STEP 2
Cook on low heat for 6-8 hours until chicken is tender and falling off the bone. Serve with your favorite veggies.

NUTRITION VALUE

625 Kcal, 20 fat,
11g fiber, 54.2g protein, 14 carbs.

CILANTRO TUNA SALAD

Tuna salad is a classic lunch option.

MAKES 2 SERVING/ TOTAL TIME 10 MINUTE

INGREDIENTS

1 can good quality tuna drained

1/4 cup olive oil

1 teaspoon sweet paprika

1 teaspoon Ground cumin

1/2 teaspoon Ground coriander

1/4 teaspoon crushed red pepper flakes

Zest and juice from 1 lime

1 clove garlic grated

1 teaspoon Grated ginger

1/4 cup chopped fresh cilantro

METHOD
STEP 1

Combine all of the ingredients in a large bowl. Mix well. Season to taste with salt and pepper. Chill until ready to serve.

NUTRITION VALUE

381 Kcal, 20g fat,
5 g fiber, 24g protein, 10g carbs.

CREAMY CAULIFLOWER AND ROOT VEGETABLE SOUP

It's creamy, flavorful, and delicious, and much better for you than the carb filled alternative. Top it with bacon for a savory salty crunch.

MAKES 4 SERVING/ TOTAL TIME 40 MINUTE

INGREDIENTS

4 slices bacon chopped

1 Onion diced

2 cloves garlic minced

2 cups Cauliflower florets

2 parsnips peeled and diced

2 turnips peeled and diced

1 teaspoon Dried thyme

6 cups Chicken broth

1 tablespoon Lemon juice

Sea salt and fresh ground pepper to taste

METHOD

STEP 1

Cook the bacon in a large soup pot until crisp. Remove with a slotted spoon. Add the onions, and garlic, and cook until soft.

Stir in the vegetables, add the thyme, and broth. Bring to a boil, reduce heat.

STEP 2

Simmer for 30 minutes until veggies are tender. Puree using a blender or immersion blender and add the lemon juice. Transfer back to pot, heat through and serve topped with reserved bacon.

NUTRITION VALUE

197 Kcal, 13g fat,
5.8g fiber, 10g protein, 14.8g carbs.

BUFFALO CHICKEN STEW

If you eat dairy, top it with a few blue cheese crumbles and chopped celery to calm your craving for buffalo wings. But if you are strict Paleo – no worries! This chicken is just as good on its own.

MAKES 4 SERVING/ TOTAL TIME 45 MINUTE

INGREDIENTS

2 tablespoons olive oil

1 Onion sliced

1 Carrot sliced

2 Stalks celery sliced

1 Red bell pepper sliced

2 cloves garlic minced

1 pound Chicken breast cubed

3-4 tablespoons Hot sauce

5 cups Chicken broth

Sea salt and fresh ground pepper to taste

METHOD

STEP 1

Heat the oil in a large soup pot and add the onion, carrot, garlic, celery, and bell peppers. Cook until soft and add the chicken. Cook until chicken is browned and add the hot sauce. Stir to mix well.

STEP 2

Add the broth and bring to a boil. Reduce to a simmer, and simmer for 30 minutes.

Serve hot, topped with desired toppings.

NUTRITION VALUE

334 Kcal, 20g fat,
0.2g fiber, 36.3g protein, 0.9g carbs.

OLIVE OIL MASHED CAULIFLOWER

You can also make this recipe come together with much less mess and time if you are able to find cauliflower that has already been riced or cut into florets.

MAKES 4 SERVING/ TOTAL TIME 30 MINUTE

INGREDIENTS

1 Head cauliflower

1/4 cup Coconut milk

1/4 cup high quality extra-virgin olive oil

1/2 teaspoon Sea salt

1/2 teaspoon Fresh ground black pepper

METHOD

STEP 1

Remove any leaves from the cauliflower and chop both the stems and florets into small pieces.
Put in a large saucepan and cover with water. Add a pinch of salt and bring to a boil. Reduce to a simmer and simmer for 15 minutes, or until very tender. Drain.

STEP 2

Add the coconut milk and olive oil and mash with a potato masher. For creamier cauliflower, use an immersion blender to puree until smooth.
Drizzle with more olive oil before serving.

NUTRITION VALUE

334 Kcal, 20g fat,
0.2g fiber, 36.3g protein, 0.9g carbs.

HEARTY FALL SALAD

The great thing about Fall is that there is an abundance of delicious fruits and vegetables that come into season.

MAKES 6 SERVING/ TOTAL TIME 30 MINUTE

INGREDIENTS

1 pound Brussels sprouts shredded

1 pear cored and diced

1 Apple cored and shredded

1/2 cup Dried cranberries

1/2 cup Toasted almonds

6 slices bacon cooked and crumbled

1/2 cup olive oil

1/4 cup Red wine vinegar

1 teaspoon molasses

1 teaspoon Dijon mustard

1/4 teaspoon Sea salt

METHOD

STEP 1

Toss the sprouts, pears, apples, cranberries, almonds, and bacon in a large bowl. Put the remaining ingredients in a jar and shake well. Toss with the salad. Chill until ready to serve.

NUTRITION VALUE

253 Kcal, 10g fat,
7g fiber, 46g protein, 15g carbs.

MAPLE PUMPKIN MEATBALLS

Eat them by themselves, paired with some veggies, or on top of some cauliflower rice.

MAKES 4 SERVING/ TOTAL TIME 45 MINUTE

INGREDIENTS

1 pound Ground beef

1/2 pound Ground pork

1/2 cup Pumpkin puree

1 Egg

1/2 cup Almond flour

1 Small onion minced

2 cloves garlic minced

1 small bunch parsley minced

1 teaspoon sea salt

1/2 teaspoon black pepper

1/4 cup Maple syrup

METHOD

STEP 1

Preheat oven to 400 degrees F.
Combine all of the ingredients except the maple syrup in a large bowl and mix well with your hands.

STEP 2

Line a baking sheet with parchment paper. Form the mixture into 2-3 inch meatballs and lay on the baking sheet. Brush the meatballs with maple syrup.
Bake for 20-25 minutes, until cooked through and browned

NUTRITION VALUE

332 Kcal, 8.7g fat,
13.6g fiber, 21g protein, 14g carbs.

GREEK CHICKEN AND VEGGIE SKEWERS

With simple ingredients and minimal prep time, you can spend less time grilling and more time soaking up the sun with your guests.

MAKES 4 SERVING/ TOTAL TIME 30 MINUTE

INGREDIENTS

1/2 cup olive oil

2 lemons, juiced

1 teaspoon Red wine vinegar

2 tablespoons Chopped fresh parsley

2 tablespoons chopped fresh mint

1 teaspoon Oregano

1/2 teaspoon Sea salt

1/2 teaspoon Fresh ground black pepper

Skewers

1.5 pounds boneless chicken cubed

1 pint Cherry tomatoes

1 Red onion cubed

2 Zucchini cubed

1 pint Button mushrooms

METHOD

STEP 1

Combine all of the marinade ingredients in a jar and shake until well combined.

Thread the chicken and vegetables onto skewers and lay in a shallow dish. Pour the marinade over top.

STEP 2

Refrigerate for at least 2 hours, turning occasionally. When ready to cook, remove the skewers from the fridge and preheat a gas or charcoal grill to medium high heat.

Grill the skewers until chicken is cooked through and veggies are lightly charred.

NUTRITION VALUE

335 Kcal, 14g fat,
8g fiber, 32g protein, 15g carbs.

Lightning Source UK Ltd.
Milton Keynes UK
UKHW050632110621
385329UK00002B/292